Emily Dickinson: The Life ... ...ous American Poet

By Cha... ...s River Editors

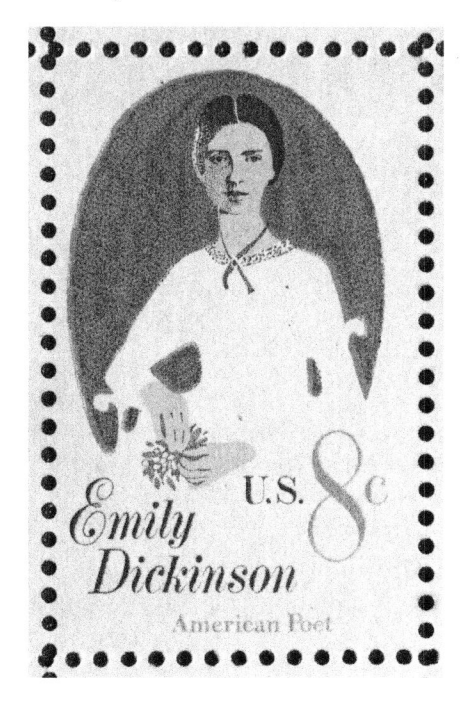

A commemorative 1971 stamp of Dickinson

About Charles River Editors

Charles River Editors is a boutique digital publishing company, specializing in bringing history back to life with educational and engaging books on a wide range of topics. Keep up to date with our new and free offerings with this 5 second sign up on our weekly mailing list, and visit Our Kindle Author Page to see other recently published Kindle titles.

We make these books for you and always want to know our readers' opinions, so we encourage you to leave reviews and look forward to publishing new and exciting titles each week.

Introduction

Emily Dickinson

"Saying nothing...sometimes says the most." – Emily Dickinson

Like many writers of her day, Emily Dickinson was a virtual unknown during her lifetime. After her death, however, when people discovered the incredible amount of poetry that she had written, Dickinson became celebrated as one of America's greatest poets.

Dickinson was notoriously introverted and mostly lived as a recluse, carrying out her friendships almost entirely by written letters. Her work was just as unique; her poetry is written with short lines, occasionally lacked titles, and often used slant rhyme and unconventional capitalization and punctuation. Only a few of her poems were published in her lifetime, but American schoolchildren across the country read her work today.

As a result, Dickinson is, even to those who have studied her the most, an enigma and, even more to the point, a contradiction. Born in an era when women rarely received more than a rudimentary education, she attended college but left before graduating. Considered by many evangelical Christians to be a pioneer of religious poetry, she struggled during her entire life to fully embrace the Calvinist doctrines taught in her New England home. She embraced the friendship of women, sometimes to a level that bordered on the obsessive, but then easily removed herself from physical contact with all but a few of her closest family members. She seemed to be, in every way, the quintessential Victorian spinster, but her poetry and letters reveal shocking passions, often shared with married men.

Not surprisingly, her poetry was just as diverse as her personal life, as she praised romantic love but criticized marriage. She wrote stanza after stanza of verse based on religious themes but never quite presented a clear cut view of the Christian faith. She produced in the same year passionate, even sexually charged verses, and also stilted observations of natural science. But in the midst of all this, she created a new genre of poetry, one that allowed her to speak her mind but in such a way that she could still move about, to the extent she wanted to, in polite society. As one writer has observed, "To make the abstract tangible, to define meaning without confining it, to inhabit a house that never became a prison, Dickinson created in her writing a distinctively elliptical language for expressing what was possible but not yet realized. Like the Concord Transcendentalists whose works she knew well, she saw poetry as a double-edged sword. While it liberated the individual, it as readily left him ungrounded." This then, proved to be both her blessing and her burden, for, left adrift, she eventually lost at least some of her grip on reality and finished her life as a mysterious recluse, not unlike a character in her own poetry.

Emily Dickinson: The Life and Legacy of the Famous American Poet looks at the reclusive life and remarkable work of the poet. Along with pictures depicting important people, places, and events, you will learn about Emily Dickinson like never before.

Emily Dickinson: The Life and Legacy of the Famous American Poet
About Charles River Editors
Introduction
   A New England Childhood
   New Influences
   A Different Path
   Poetry
   Online Resources
   Bibliography
Free Books by Charles River Editors
Discounted Books by Charles River Editors

A New England Childhood

"God is sitting here, looking into my very soul to see if I think right thoughts. Yet I am not afraid, for I try to be right and good; and He knows every one of my struggles." – Emily Dickinson, 1850

Emily Elizabeth Dickinson was born on December 10, 1830 in Amherst, Massachusetts, to Edward Dickinson, a young lawyer striving to establish himself in New England politics, and his wife, the former Emily Norcross. The home in which the infant Emily first opened her eyes belonged not to her parents, for they were still too young and poor to have purchased a home of their own, but to her paternal grandfather, Samuel Fowler Dickinson, the founder of the family's legal firm, where Edward also worked. Little Emily would grow up as the family's "middle child," with her brother, Edward, Jr., about a year and a half older, and her sister, Lavinia ("Vinnie"), who would join the family in 1833.

Dickinson's home

Edward Dickinson

    It is likely that Emily's mother was one of the main driving forces behind her writing. The older Emily enjoyed writing, and she had also attended the co-educational Monson Academy in Massachusetts for 12 years, longer than most any woman in the early 19th century would have been educated. Not surprisingly, she encouraged her children to be scholarly. She also boarded for a year at a school in New Haven, Connecticut before returning home to help her mother with her eight younger siblings. Three years later, she began a relationship with Edward Dickinson, and the two married in May 1828.

    When Emily was seven years old, her father finally realized the first of his political ambitions when he was elected to the Massachusetts State Legislature, where he served for two years before returning to his legal practice. He next served in the Massachusetts State Senate in 1842 and 1843. Again, he left politics, this time for a decade, after which he served a term as Massachusetts's Representative in Congress.

Whether their father was serving away or at home, the three Dickinson children's lives remained much the same. All three began their educations at Amherst Academy, the original home of Amherst College. Though Austin later transferred to Williston Seminary, the sisters remained at Amherst for their entire educations. Though this may seem inconsistent with Dickinson's own mother's education, Amherst Academy was in every way a superior school for young women, allowing (and even encouraging) its students to attend lectures on the college campus.

The Dickinson children, with Emily on the left

Like her mother before her, Emily developed quite an interest in the sciences. She wrote to a friend when she was 14 years old, "My plants look finely now. I am going to send you a little geranium leaf, which you must press for me. Have you made an herbarium yet? ... Most all the girls are making one. If you do, perhaps I can make some additions to it from flowers growing around here.... I have been to walk tonight and got some very choice wild flowers...I have four studies. They are Mental Philosophy, Geology, Latin and Botany." Fortunately, Emily found in her textbook, *Familiar Lectures on Botany* by Almira Hart Lincoln Phelps, a way to unite science, at least in the form of Nature Studies, with the other two great passions of her life: poetry and religion. In the book, Phelps wrote, "The study of nature in any of her varieties is highly interesting and useful. ... The vegetable world offers a boundless field of inquiry, which may be explored with the most pure and delightful emotions. Here the Almighty seems to manifest himself to us with less of that dazzling sublimity which it is almost painful to behold in His more magnificent creations; and it might almost appear, that accommodating the vegetable world to our capacities, He had especially designed it for our investigation and amusement...The study of Botany naturally leads to greater love and reverence for the Deity. We would not affirm that it does in reality always produce this effect; for, unhappily, there are some minds which, though quick to perceive the beauties of nature, seem, blindly, to overlook Him who spread them forth. They can admire the gifts, while they forget the Giver. But those who feel in their hearts a love to God, and who see in the natural world the workings of His power, can look abroad, and adopting the language of a Christian poet, exclaim, 'My Father made them all.'"

Phelps

Phelps' respect of the dignity and worth of every species matched Dickinson's own views, and the latter would never embrace the world of destructive research, preferring instead the romanticized view of nature. In fact, she complained in her poem "Arcturus' is his other name," that "[i]t's very mean of Science/To go and interfere!"

> "I slew a worm the other day—
> A 'Savant' passing by
> Murmured 'Resurgam'—'Centipede'!
> 'Oh Lord—how frail are we'!
>
> I pull a flower from the woods—
> A monster with a glass
> Computes the stamens in a breath—

And has her in a 'class'!

Whereas I took the Butterfly
Aforetime in my hat—
He sits erect in 'Cabinets'—
The Clover bells forgot. "

…

"What once was 'Heaven'
Is 'Zenith' now—
Where I proposed to go
When Time's brief masquerade was done
Is mapped and charted too.

What if the poles should frisk about
And stand upon their heads!
I hope I'm ready for 'the worst'—
Whatever prank betides!

Perhaps the 'Kingdom of Heaven's' changed—
I hope the 'Children' there Won't be 'new fashioned' when I come—
And laugh at me—and stare—

I hope the Father in the skies
Will lift his little girl—
Old fashioned—naught—everything—
Over the stile of 'Pearl.'"

  Though most of her classes emphasized the importance of the sciences, Dickinson had the good fortune during her time at Amherst to be able to learn from Leonard Humphrey. According to Dickinson biographer Mabel Todd, Humphrey "graduated from Amherst [College] as valedictorian in 1846, being subsequently Principal of the well-known Amherst Academy, and still later a theological student at Andover, and tutor in Amherst College. His sudden death on November 30, 1850 caused much grief to his many friends, who admired his polished scholarship and lovable personality." Following his death, Dickinson mourned, writing that "some of my friends are gone, and some of my friends are sleeping – sleeping the churchyard sleep – the hour of evening is sad – it was once my study hour – my master has gone to rest, and the open leaf of the book, and the scholar at school alone, make the tears come, and I cannot brush them away ; I would not if I could, for they are the only tribute I can pay the departed Humphrey. You have stood by the grave before; I have walked there sweet summer evenings and read the names on the stones, and wondered who would come and give me the same memorial; but I never have laid my friends there, and forgot that they too must die; this is my first affliction, and indeed 'tis hard to bear it."

While Humphrey was perhaps Dickinson's first "Master," he was far from her last. While at Ahmert, she began to cultivate a group of peers that would continue to inspire her writing for much of her life. She was also enjoying a rare sense of independence unavailable to most women of her generation, although more common to those of her class. While at school, she was able to form ideas and relationships separate from those of her family, and such connections were encouraged by many middle-class parents who supported these brief periods of freedom that lay between childhood and marriage.

Dickinson was fortunate enough to have more of this kind of time, because after she graduated from Amherst, she entered Mount Holyoke Female Seminary in 1847. The school's founder, Mary Lyon, offered a rigorous curriculum designed to mold both the minds and souls of her young charges, as Dickinson detailed in a letter home to her family. "At six o'clock we all rise. We breakfast at 7. Our study hour begins at 8. At 9 we all meet at Seminary Hall for devotions. At 10.15 I recite a review of Ancient History in connection with which we read Goldsmith and Grimshaw. At 11 I recite a lesson on Pope's Essay on Man, which is merely transposition. At 12 I practise calisthenics, and at 12.15 I read until dinner which is at 12.30. After dinner from 1.30 till 2, I sing in Seminary Hall. From 2.45 till 3.45 I practise upon the piano. At 3.45 I go to Sections, where we give all our accounts for the day; including absence, tardiness, communications, breaking silence, study hours, receiving company in our rooms and ten thousand other things which I will not take time to mention."

Lyon

Away from their families, these young women enjoyed the nearly unheard of freedom to make their own decisions about such life-shaping matters as religion, but with freedom came the inevitable burden of responsibility, and Dickinson found it a heavy one, for while she longed for some sort of connection to the divine, she was unwilling to simply go along with the doctrines of those around her. This situation came to a head during her first term at Mount Holyoke, since Lyon considered herself the guardian of her scholars' souls, a position she took very seriously. Each week she questioned her students on their religious beliefs, classifying some as "established Christians," others who "expressed hope" for salvation, and a few whom she considered "without hope." According to Clara Newman Turner, who knew Dickinson personally, one day, "Miss Lyon, during a time of religious interest in the school, asked all those who wanted to be Christians to rise. The wording of the request was not such as Emily could honestly accede to and she remained seated—the only one who did not rise. In relating the incident to me, she said, 'They thought it queer I didn't rise'—adding with a twinkle in her eye, 'I thought a lie would be queerer.'" Thus, Dickinson was given the dreaded "without hope" label.

New Influences

"If I read a book [and] it makes my whole body so cold no fire can ever warm me, I know that is poetry. If I feel physically as if the top of my head were taken off, I know that is poetry. These are the only ways I know it. Is there any other way?" – Emily Dickinson, 1870

Dickinson as a young woman

Dickinson left Mount Holyoke just a few months later, not because of any spiritual affliction, but because of a physical one. Writing to Root in May 1848, she complained, "I had not been very well all winter, but had not written home about it, lest the folks should take me home. During the week following examinations, a friend from Amherst came over and spent a week with me, and when that friend returned home, father and mother were duly notified of the state of my health. ...Saturday of the same week Austin arrived in full sail, with orders from headquarters to bring me home at all events. ... You must not imbibe the idea from what I have said that I do not love home - far from it. But I could not bear to leave teachers and companions before the close of the term and go home to be dosed and receive the physician daily, and take warm drinks and be condoled with on the state of health in general by all the old ladies in the town."

Apparently her parents made the right decision. She added, "I was dosed for about a month after my return home, without any mercy, till at last out of mere pity my cough went away, and I had quite a season of peace. Thus I remained at home until the close of the term, comforting my parents by my presence, and instilling many a lesson of wisdom into the budding intellect of my only sister. I had almost forgotten to tell you that I went on with my studies at home, and kept up with my class. Last Thursday our vacation closed, and on Friday morn, midst the weeping of friends, crowing of roosters, and singing of birds, I again took my departure from home."

Alas, she was not to remain at school. She concluded, "Father has decided not to send me to Holyoke another year, so this is my last term. Can it be possible that I have been here almost a year? It startles me when I really think of the advantages I have had, and I fear I have not improved them as I ought. But many an hour has fled with its report to heaven, and what has been the tale of me?"

Fortunately, she learned to take comfort in the written word, and this lesson brought her much comfort. She had written her first published piece back at Amherst. Called "Magnum bonum, harem scarum," it was published in *The Indicator* on "Valentine Eve" in 1850. In it, she wrote, "Sir, I desire an interview; meet me at sunrise, or sunset, or the new moon—the place is immaterial. In gold, or in purple, or sacklosh—I look not upon the raiment. With sword, or with pen or with plough—the weapons are less than the wielder. In coach, or in wagon, or walking, the equipage far from the man. With soul, or spirit, or body, they are all alike to me. With host or alone, in sunshine or storm, in heaven or earth, somehow or no hoe—I propose, sir, to see you."

From there, Dickinson meandered through a discussion of the United States ("so hurrah for North Carolina, since we are on this point"), a dog, ("The Dog is the noblest work of Art, sir") and "Alms-houses, and transcendental State prisons, and scaffolds."

Later, in 1852, the *Springfield Daily Republican* published "'Sic transit gloria mundi,'" meaning "Thus passes the glory of this world." In the beginning, it is difficult to tell if this is a poem or a Latin exercise, as it begins:

>"Sic transit gloria mundi,'
>'How doth the busy bee,'
>'Dum vivimus vivamus,'
>I stay mine enemy!
>
>Oh 'veni, vidi, vici!'
>Oh caput cap-a-pie!
>And oh 'memento mori'
>When I am far from thee!"

From here she moved on to praise Peter Parley, Daniel Boone, and "the gentleman Who first observed the moon!" In fact, the poem reads more like a nursery rhyme or schoolyard chant than the transcendental pieces she would later compose. She put much of her efforts into detailing small snippets of knowledge she gleaned at school: "During my education,/It was announced to me/That gravitation, stumbling,/Fell from an apple tree!...It was the brave Columbus,/A sailing o'er the tide,/Who notified the nations/Of where I would reside!"

The work concludes with the following:

"In token of our friendship
Accept this "Bonnie Doon,"
And when the hand that plucked it
Hath passed beyond the moon,

The memory of my ashes
Will consolation be;
Then, farewell, Tuscarora,
And farewell, Sir, to thee!"

   The 1850s marked a time of continual loss for Dickinson, as one after another of her friends from school and other places married and became consumed with their new duties as wives and mothers. Inevitably, letters to her old school friends received fewer replies, so she turned to new sources of entertainment, usually in the form of books. This proved to be a boon to her own writing, as she became more and more acquainted with the works of others. She read much older works, such as the Bible and Shakespeare, but also contemporaneous works by the likes of Ralph Waldo Emerson and Henry Wadsworth Longfellow. Up until this point in her life, much of her reading had been limited to titles either assigned by her schoolmasters or approved by her father, but now she was a young adult who could choose her own reading material. As author Domhnall Mitchell noted, "Even if she read almost indiscriminately, she had a keenly developed (and, judging by the list of names, a culturally conservative) sense of what did and did not constitute literary merit and importance. Like many of her day, she operated with a vertical model of writerly excellence, and, rather like a pyramid, it had a broad base and a narrow top. Like pyramids, the best books immortalized the minds of their creators, and, as her sister, Vinnie, once said, Dickinson was very discriminating: she was 'always watching for the rewarding person'--in literature as in life. Her judgments about which monuments best preserved the memory of their architects did not always coincide with that of the literary cultural establishment, but generally speaking George Eliot, Charles Dickens, Robert and Elizabeth Barrett Browning, and the Brontë sisters represented a kind of literary aristocracy for her, whereas she had problems acknowledging the value of someone like Whitman--who was 'disgraceful.'"

Emerson

Longfellow

Mitchell was also quick to point out that Dickinson was not a literary snob: "This is not to say that British writers influenced Dickinson more than American ones: the work of Sewall, Karl Keller, David S. Reynolds, and Joanne Dobson, among others, argues the very strong links between Dickinson and (some of) her contemporaries. But it is to say that (especially in her later years) she admired more British writers than she did American ones…Dickinson's list of names is significant because, in the context of contemporaneous literary debate, it seems to align her with a Whiggish or conservative faction of American intellectuals who advocated an aristocratic and pro-British theory of literature in opposition to those who favored a democratic and national ideal…"

At the same time, however, Mitchell noted the different ways Dickinson conveyed thoughts, and how different characters in her works might not accurately represent what she personally thought. "A number of Dickinson poems would appear to support this possibility, while her preoccupation with images of royalty and various forms of nobility would also appear to suggest that she may at times have agreed with establishment and elitist definitions of the artist and her or his function…her 'posthumous' poems…that are spoken by a persona who is clearly dead, remind us that her work often involves a dramatization of psychic and social possibilities that should not be literally translated as representing her exact views. …W. A. Jones…could write that 'democratic as we are, we yet contend right loyally and reverently, for the sovereignty of mind, the aristocracy of genius, the high rank and precedence of talent.' Nevertheless, Jones believed that the highest forms of poetry would be essentially philanthropic, whereas Dickinson's poetry does not appear to take an interest in bettering or even describing social environments."

In addition to the published works that she read during this period of her life, Dickinson's current and future works were also shaped by constructive criticism and words of encouragement that she received from personal friends in letters. Among these correspondents was Samuel Bowles, editor-in-chief of the *Springfield Republican*. Rumored to have been something of a womanizer, Bowles may not have been the most appropriate correspondent for a single woman, but regardless, she wrote a rather flirtatious letter to him in 1853: "I would like to have you dwell here. Though it is almost nine o'clock, the skies are gay and yellow, and there's a purple craft or so, in which a friend could sail. Tonight looks like 'Jerusalem.' I think Jerusalem must be like Sue's Drawing Room, when we are talking and laughing there, and you and Mrs Bowles are by. I hope we may all behave so as to reach Jerusalem. How are your Hearts today? Ours are pretty well. I hope your tour was bright, and gladdened Mrs. Bowles. Perhaps the Retrospect will call you back some morning. You shall find us all at the gate, if you come in a hundred years, just as we stood that day. … I rode with Austin this morning. He showed me mountains that touched the sky, and brooks that sang like Bobolinks. Was he not very kind? I will give them to you, for they are mine and 'all things are mine' excepting 'Cephas and Apollos,' for whom I have no taste."

Bowles

It was perhaps through Bowles that Dickinson met Josiah Holland, who was also an editor with the *Republican*. Her correspondence with him was more circumspect, and she addressed most of her letters to his wife, Mary, with whom she shared some of her religious struggles. In November 1854, Dickinson wrote to Mary, "The minister to-day, not our own minister, preached about death and judgment, and what would become of those, meaning Austin and me, who behaved improperly - and somehow the sermon scared me, and father and Vinnie looked very solemn as if the whole was true, and I would not for worlds have them know that I troubled me, but I longed to come to you, and tell you all about it, and learn how to be better. He preached such an awful sermon though, that I didn't much think I should ever see you again until Judgment Day, and then you would not speak to me, according to his story. The subject of perdition seemed to please him, somehow. It seems very solemn to me. I'll tell you all about it, when I see you again."

Holland

Eventually, the two men proved to be huge assets by publishing several of her poems, including "Nobody knows this little rose."

"Nobody knows this little Rose—

It might a pilgrim be

Did I not take it from the ways

And lift it up to thee.

Only a Bee will miss it—

Only a Butterfly,

Hastening from far journey—

On its breast to lie—

Only a Bird will wonder—

Only a Breeze will sigh—

Ah Little Rose—how easy

For such as thee to die! Nobody knows this little Rose—

It might a pilgrim be

Did I not take it from the ways

And lift it up to thee.

Only a Bee will miss it—

Only a Butterfly,

Hastening from far journey—

On its breast to lie—

Only a Bird will wonder—

Only a Breeze will sigh—

Ah Little Rose—how easy

For such as thee to die!"

When their father left them in Massachusetts to serve in Congress in 1853, Emily and her sister Vinnie spent much of their time traveling, either to see Josiah and Mary Holland or their father in Washington. On one occasion in 1855, they stayed with Eliza Coleman, an old friend of Emily's from Amherst. While there, they attended church with Coleman and heard a sermon preached by the Reverend Charles Wadsworth, a pastor famous for both his preaching and the way in which he cared for his flock. Dickinson soon found herself drawn to him and later declared that he was one of the "Masters" who had so influenced her life. Historians are not sure whether Dickinson ever wrote to Wadsworth directly but she would, from time to time, send letters to Holland with a request that she forward them to Wadsworth.

Of course, it's easy to wonder why Dickinson would use such a sly way to communicate with a man obviously accustomed to corresponding with and counseling both men and women. None of these letters survive, and nobody would have known they ever existed at all if Dickinson had not mentioned them in extant letters between her and Holland. Was she in love with him? Did he reciprocate her feelings? A certain answer could never be known, but there are tantalizing clues. In the only surviving letter from him to her, he addressed her as, "My dear Miss Dickenson" and wrote, "I am distressed beyond measure at your note, received this moment–I can only imagine the affliction which has befallen, or is now befalling you. Believe me, be what it may, you have all my sympathy, and my constant, earnest prayers. I am very, very anxious to learn more definitely of your trial–and though I have no right to intrude upon your sorrow, I beg you to write me, though it be but a word– In great haste…" At the end, he signed it, "Sincerely and most affectionately yours," indicating that they shared a relationship closer than that which he might share with an occasional visitor to his church.

There are three letters in the collection of Dickinson's correspondence that were never sent and do not feature the name of the intended recipient, but some scholars believe that these were intended for Wadsworth. One of these contains words that seem to speak of a resolve to remain chastely faithful to him until some future date when their love can be fulfilled. "If it had been God's will that I might breathe where you breathed–and find the place–myself–at night–if I never forget that I am not with you…to come nearer than presbyteries–and nearer than the new Coat–that the tailor made…is forbidden me…. I used to think when I died I could see you–so I died as fast as I could–but the "Corporation" are going to heaven too so [Eternity] won't be sequestered –now–say I may wait for you–say I need go with no stranger to the to me untried fold–I waited a long time–master–but I can wait more–wait til my hazel hair is dappled–and you carry the cane–then I can look at my watch–and if the day is too far declined–we can take the chances for heaven–what would you do with me if I came 'in white'? Have you a little chest to put the Alive–in? I want to see you more–Sir–than all I wish for in this world."

On the other hand, during this same time period, Dickinson wrote the following to her recognized suitor and potential lover, Judge Otis Phillips Lord: "Incarcerate me in yourself–that will punish me–Threading with you this lovely maze which is not Life or death tho it has the intangibleness of one and the flush of the other waking for your sake on day made magical with you before I went to sleep–what pretty phrase–we went to sleep as if it were a country–let us make it one-we could make it one, my native land–my darling come oh be a patriot now–Love is a patriot now gave her life for its country." Thus, it seems more likely that the mysterious drafts were intended for him, not Wadsworth.

Lord, 18 years Dickinson's senior, was a close friend and political ally of Edward Dickinson. He often visited the Dickinson home with his wife, Elizabeth, especially during the years leading up to his appointment to the Massachusetts Superior Court in 1859. While it is generally accepted that his and Emily's feelings for each other only blossomed into romance after

Elizabeth died in 1877, there is some evidence that their relationship began much earlier. In fact, biographer John Evangelist Walsh claimed, "If Emily had never met the married Otis Lord, certainly her personal life, and perhaps also her career as a poet, would have been very different. Never would she have become a recluse but very probably would have married and raised a family. For some, the picture of the supposedly ethereal Emily having a husband to care for and babies to tend is distasteful, in its way shocking. But we are speaking here of real life, not the subtle, too often distorting charm of literary fantasy. Was she, we may pointedly ask, ever really happy in shutting herself off from the world, keeping life in its fullness at arm's length? 'She hated her peculiarities,' said her closest friend, her sister-in-law Susan, 'and shrank from any notice of them.' Susan, if anyone did, knew the truth.'

At the same time, Walsh acknowledges that due to the standards of the day, there is little reason to believe their relationship ever became physical. "As for what they did or didn't do, as to physical intimacy…only speculation can suggest. The one bit of evidence is found in a letter Emily wrote to Lord years later, and it seems to be against any full sexual encounter." Walsh is referring to a letter Emily wrote in 1880, in which she confessed, "It is strange that I miss you so much at night, when I was never with you---but the punctual love invokes you soon as my eyes are shut---and I wake warm with the want sleep had almost filled---I dreamed last week that you had died, and one had carved a statue of you and I was asked to unveil it, and I said that what I had not done in life I would not in death when your loved eyes could not forgive."

One of the aspects of her personality that seems to have been causing Dickinson a strange mixture of pride and concern was the way in which she found her own thoughts and feelings at odds with those of other women her own age. Indeed, as she looked around, she came to feel that there was something a little bit strange about her entire family. Within a letter full of family and local gossip, she mused to her brother Austin, "The Newmans seem very pleasant, but they are not like us. What makes a few of us so different from others? It's a question I often ask myself. The Germanians gave a concert here, the evening of Exhibition day. Vinnie and I went with John. I never heard [such] sounds before. They seemed like brazen Robins, all wearing broadcloth wings, and I think they were, for they all flew away as soon as the concert was over."

A Different Path

Dickinson as an adult

"Success is counted sweetest / By those who ne'er succeed." – Emily Dickinson, "Success is counted sweetest"

Upon returning home, Dickinson found it difficult to subjugate her intellectual interests to the needs of her family, as was expected of her. During the 1850s, she wrote a number of letters in which she complained about both her lack of interest and skill in domestic duties. She wrote to one friend, "I tell you I have been dreaming, dreaming a golden dream, with eyes all the while wide open, and I guess it's almost morning; and besides, I have been at work, providing the 'food that perisheth,' scaring the timorous dust, and being obedient and kind. I am yet the Queen of the Court, if regalia be dust and dirt, have three loyal subjects, whom I 'd rather relieve from service. Mother is still an invalid, though a partially restored one; father and Austin still clamor for food; and I, like a martyr, am feeding them. Wouldn't you love to see me in these bonds of great despair, looking around my kitchen, and praying for kind deliverance, and declaring by 'Omai's beard' I never was in such plight ? My kitchen, I think I called it — God forbid that it was, or shall be, my own — God keep me from what they call households, except that bright one of 'faith'!...Don't be afraid of my imprecations — they never did any one harm, and they make me feel so cool, and so very much more comfortable ! ...save me a little sheaf, only a very little one! Remember and care for me sometimes, and scatter a fragrant flower in this wilderness life of mine by writing me…"

One of the most trying aspects of Emily's life was the constant round of calls she was expected to both make and receive. Visiting in homes was in some ways the very fabric of 19th century American life, and Emily was expected, in the absence of her invalid mother, to have "at home" days in which she received visitors, as well as days when she herself went out to visit others, often for no reasons other than the fact that they had visited her. While some of these visits, such as those to and from old school friends, were welcome, many, made on behalf of her father to his political connections, were not. Ultimately, Dickinson rebelled by passing the visiting duties down to Vinnie.

During the 1850s, Amherst became caught up in the religious revival sweeping the nation. Not only did local ministers redouble their efforts to bring lost sheep into the fold, they also brought in visiting ministers with reputations for fiery oratory and hard hitting sermons that threatened the unrepentant with eternal damnation. Their words took hold in Austin's family, and Edward joined the church in August 1850, followed by Vinnie in November. Austin and Emily, on the other hand, still resisted, and she wrote to her longtime friend and confidant, Jane Humphrey, in April 1850, "Christ is calling everyone here, all my companions have answered, even my darling Vinnie believes she loves, and trusts him, and I am standing alone in rebellion, and growing very careless. Abby, Mary, Jane, and farthest of all my Vinnie have been seeking, and they all believe they have found; I can't tell you what they have found, but they think it is something precious. I wonder if it is?...How strange is this sanctification, that works such a marvellous change, that sows in such corruption, and rises in golden glory, that brings Christ down, and shews him, and lets him select his friends! In the day time it seems like Sundays, and I wait for the bell to ring, and at evening a great deal stranger, the 'still small voice' grows earnest and rings, and returns, and lingers, and the faces of good men shine, and bright halos come around them; and the eyes of the disobedient look down, and become ashamed. It certainly comes from God - and I think to receive it is blessed - not that I know it from me, but from those on whom change has passed. They seem so very tranquil, and their voices are kind, and gentle, and the tears fill their eyes so often, I really think I envy them."

While religion figured prominently in Dickinson's thoughts and concerns during this period, she had other things on her mind as well, primarily poetry. She was learning to wrestle with herself and her outlook on life through writing, and she began to attempt to hone her craft, reading and re-reading a volume of poetry by Emerson. She wrote as much as possible each day, penning long meandering letters to family and friends. To her closest and most trusted correspondents she gained permission to write in the character of someone other than herself, sometimes as a fictional heroine from a favorite novel, and other times as an angry narrator critiquing the world around her.

Among her closest confidants at that time was a young woman named Susan Gilbert. A mere nine days younger than Dickinson, she was also a daughter of Massachusetts, having grown up in nearby Deerfield. The two met in 1850 when Austin brought Susan home to meet his family, and she and Emily formed an instant bond, based largely on their mutual love for poetry. Dickinson wrote of and to her constantly, sending her many pieces of her own work to critique, and discussing those written by others. Late in 1850, she observed to Gilbert, "Longfellow's 'golden Legend' has come to town I hear -- and may be seen in state on Mr. Adams' bookshelves. …for our sakes dear Susie, who please ourselves with the fancy that we are the only poets -- and everyone else is prose, let us hope they will yet be willing to share our humble world and feed upon such aliment as we consent to do!"

Harvard University, Houghton Library, w99707_1

Susan Gilbert

It should come as no surprise to anyone that two such passionate people who constantly discuss polarizing topics would ultimately reach a disagreement, and this eventually happened between Dickinson and Gilbert. In 1854, Dickinson's temper reached such a state that she wrote to Gilbert, "Sue - you can go or stay - There is but one alternative - We differ often lately, and this must be the last. You need not fear to leave me lest I should be alone, for I often part with things

I fancy I have loved, sometimes to the grave, and sometimes to an oblivion rather bitterer than death -- thus my heart bleeds so frequently that I shant mind the hemorrhage, and I can only add an agony to several previous ones, and at the end of day remark - a bubble burst! Such incidents would grieve me when I was but a child, and perhaps I could have wept when little feet hard by mine, stood still in the coffin, but eyes grow dry sometimes, and hearts get crisp and cinder, and had as lief burn."

Perhaps enjoying the drama of the moment, Dickinson continued, perhaps bating Gilbert, for whom religious faith was a priority: "[T]hough in that last day, the Jesus Christ you love, remark he does not know me - there is a darker spirit will not disown its child. Few have been given me, and if I love them so, that for idolatry, they are removed from me - I simply murmur gone, and the billow dies away into the boundless blue, and no one knows but me, that one went down today. We have walked very pleasantly – Perhaps this is the point at which our paths diverge...."

Dickinson then concluded with this somewhat flippant poem:

"I have a Bird in spring
Which for myself doth sing -
The spring decoys.
And as the summer nears -
And as the Rose appears,
Robin is gone.

"Yet do I not repine
Knowing that Bird of mine
Though flown -
Learneth beyond the sea
Melody new for me
And will return.

"Fast in a safer hand
Held in a truer Land
Are mine -
And though they now depart,
Tell I my doubting heart
They're thine.

"In a serener Bright,
In a more golden light
I see
Each little doubt and fear,

> each little discord here
> Removed.
>
> "Then will I not repine,
> Knowing that Bird of mine
> Though flown
> Shall in a distant tree
> Bright melody for me
> Return."

Much has been made of the intimate words exchanged between Dickinson and Gilbert, fueling theories about their feelings towards each other, but the language that Dickinson used in her correspondence with Gilbert is not that different from the way in which she wrote to several of her other friends. Indeed, it was consistent with the way many Victorian women of her class and education communicated with each other, so reading sexuality into it would be to make the all too common mistake of applying 21st century cultural standards to 19th century practices.

While the women shared many similar outlooks on life, one of the ways in which they differed was on the important topic of marriage. Dickinson held the institution in suspicion, and often expressed her opinion that the role of wife was not something that any intelligent woman would embrace with joy. At the same time, she was fully aware that marriage was desired by most women her age, as she conceded in a letter written to Gilbert in June 1852, shortly after Gilbert's engagement to Dickinson's brother. "I don't know why it is -- but there's something in your name, now you are taken from me, which fills my heart so full, and my eye, too. ... Mattie was here last evening, and we sat on the front door stone, and talked about life and love, and whispered our childish fancies about such blissful things -- the evening was gone so soon, and I walked home with Mattie beneath the silent moon, and wished for you…. You did not come…as we walked side by side and wondered if that great blessedness which may be our's sometime, is granted now, to some. Those unions, my dear Susie, by which two lives are one, this sweet and strange adoption wherein we can but look, and are not yet admitted, how it can fill the heart, and make it gang wildly beating, how it will take us one day, and make us all it's own, and we shall not run away from it, but lie still and be happy!"

Revealing to her closest friend her ambivalence, she continued, "How dull our lives must seem to the bride, and the plighted maiden, whose days are fed with gold, and who gathers pearls every evening; but to the wife, Susie, sometimes the wife forgotten, our lives perhaps seem dearer than all others in the world…you have seen flowers at morning, satisfied with the dew, and those same sweet flowers at noon with their heads bowed in anguish before the mighty sun; think you these thirsty blossoms will now need naught but - dew? No, they will cry for sunlight, and pine for the burning noon, tho' it scorches them, scathes them; they have got through with peace - they know that the man of noon, is mightier than the morning and their life is henceforth to him. Oh, Susie, it is dangerous, and it is all too dear, these simple trusting spirits, and the spirits mightier, which we cannot resist! It does so rend me, Susie, the thought of it when it comes, that I tremble lest at sometime I, too, am yielded up."

Edward Dickinson lost his bid for re-election in 1855 and thus returned home disappointed. Finding comfort, as always, through his family, he returned to practicing law, this time taking Austin on as a full partner. While Dickinson eschewed many domestic expectations, there is one which she embraced with fervor, that of trusted guide and confidant to her brother. 19th Century society saw women as the moral forces in families, and so Emily was encouraged to prevail upon her brother, though he was older, to choose a righteous path in life, in spite of the many temptations around him. In a letter dated March 27, 1853, she wrote happily, "How thankful we should be that you have been brought to Greenville, and a suitable frame of mind! I really had my doubts about your reaching Canaan, but you relieve my mind, and set me at rest completely. How long it is since you've been in this state of complacence towards God and your fellow men? I think it must be sudden, hope you are not deceived, would recommend 'Pilgrim's Progress,' and 'Baxter upon the will.' Hope you have enjoyed the Sabbath, and sanctuary privileges - it is'nt all young men that have the preached word. Trust you enjoy your closet, and meditate profoundly upon the Daily Food! I shall send you Village Hymns, by earliest opportunity. I was just this moment thinking of a favorite stanza of your's 'where congregations ne'er break up, and Sabbaths have no end.' That must be a delightful situation, certainly, quite worth the scrambling for!"

Austin may have been approaching a state of grace at this point, but he had not yet reached it, at least not in the eyes of the religious establishment. In fact, would be several more years before he joined a church, and his ongoing moral lassitude can be seen in Dickinson's other remarks. She later upbraided him teasingly, "I suppose you will go to the 'Hygeum' as usual, this evening. Think it a dreadful thing for a young man under influences to frequent a hotel, evenings! Am glad our Pilgrim Fathers got safely out of the way, before such shocking times! Are you getting on well with 'the work,' and have you engaged the Harpers? Shall bring in a bill for my Lead Pencils, 17, in number, disbursed at times to you, as soon as the publishment. Also, two envelopes daily, during despatch of proofs, also Johnnie Beston, also David Smith, and services from same! Dear Austin, I am keen, but you are a good deal keener, I am something of a fox, but you are more of a hound! I guess we are very good friends tho', and I guess we both love Sue just as well as we can."

Indeed, Dickinson was thrilled when Austin finally married Gilbert. By this time, the family had moved back to the Homestead, where the children had been born. Emily loved the house and had often visited there during Edward's time in Washington. According to biographer Martha Dickinson, "Emily's only brother, Austin, was married on July 1, 1856, and from that time she was part of every incident in his household. Her first little note to his wife, with which 'The Single Hound' is prefaced, expressed her feeling perfectly:

'One sister have I in our house
And one a hedge away --
There's only one recorded
But both belong to me.'"

Martha continued, "[H]er brother's marriage brought a thrilling new element into her life, and she continued to flit across the intervening lawns behind the bulwark of high hemlock hedges long after all other visits had definitely ceased. The narrow path 'just wide enough for two who love' ran luringly between, whether her light flashed across the snow to them under a polar moon, while she sat up to watch over her flowers and keep them from freezing, or past the rosebushes of a midsummer, where the moths were at their amorous trafficking."

The Evergreens, Austin and Susan's home

By the time Susan and Austin married, Dickinson herself was 26 years old and, while there were certainly still the hope in the minds of her friends and families, if not her own, that she might marry, she was most likely classified by those around her as an "old maid." This would be a difficult label for any Victorian era woman to endure, but for someone with Dickinson's gifts and education, it rankled on a different level, because she had to constantly question whether she had arrived at this point through her own choices. More importantly, she had to face the ongoing question of how she felt about those choices, and whether she was satisfied with her life as it stood then and would likely stand in the future.

Around this time, Dickinson's demeanor was slowly changing, as she was beginning to succumb to the mysterious desire for isolation that would shape the remainder of her life. For one thing, she became very possessive of her friends, writing to Bowles in 1858, "My friends are my 'estate.' Forgive me then the avarice to hoard them! They tell me those were poor early, have different views of gold. I don't know how that is. God is not so wary as we, else he would give us no friends, lest we forget him! The charms of the Heaven in the bush are superseded I fear, by the Heaven in the hand, occasionally."

More significantly, Dickinson became more focused on death and mourning, spending hours comforting friends who had suffered losses ranging from stillborn children to aged parents. She wrote to one friend, a minister who had lost his wife, "I do not ask if you are 'better'---because split lives---never 'get well'---but the love of friends---sometimes helps the Staggering---when the heart had on it's great freight."

Dickinson became something of a self-appointed comforter, as one author, writing for the Poetry Foundation, observed: "In these years, she turned increasingly to the cryptic style that came to define her writing. The letters are rich in aphorism and dense with allusion. She asks her reader to complete the connection her words only imply—to round out the context from which the allusion is taken, to take the part and imagine a whole. Through her letters, Dickinson reminds her correspondents that their broken worlds are not a mere chaos of fragments. Behind the seeming fragments of her short statements lies the invitation to remember the world in which each correspondent shares a certain and rich knowledge with the other. They alone know the extent of their connections; the friendship has given them the experiences peculiar to the relation."

It seems that comforting others may have become an all-consuming task for Dickinson, to the extent that she began to remove herself from the company of friends who were not caught up in tragedies. In 1858, she wrote to her cousin, Louise Norcross, "For you remember, dear, you are one of the ones from whom I do not run away! That is remarkable in itself."

What caused this slow decline into solitude? It is difficult to say. Some authors feel that it must in some way be related to a failed or unrequited love, while others believe that it was a practical decision made by a woman who did not want to bother making and receiving calls. Still others point to some sort of mental illness as the cause, citing either depression or agoraphobia. In fact, it could have a combination of any or all of these reasons, and it is possible that even Dickinson herself did not understand the cause.

However, it is clear that by withdrawing from people, she threw herself more fanatically into her writing, making the 1860s her most productive decade.

An 1859 daguerreotype believed to be of Dickinson and her friend Kate Scott Turner

Poetry

"Because I could not stop for Death -

He kindly stopped for me -

The Carriage held but just Ourselves -

And Immortality." – Emily Dickinson, "Because I could not stop for Death"

By the late 1850s and early 1860s, Dickinson began to take the fate of her works into her own hands, giving up, for the most part, her efforts to get them published. Writing from Pennsylvania State University in 1995, Dorothy Huff Oberhaus noted, "Although the poems of Emily Dickinson remained virtually unpublished during her lifetime, she did engage in a private kind of self-publication from about 1858 to 1864. During those years, she made copies of more than eight hundred of her poems, gathered them into forty groups, and bound each of these gatherings together with string to form booklets. While she sometimes sent a friend a copy of one of the poems from the booklets, there is no evidence that she showed them in their bound form to anyone."

In the years following Dickinson's death, the fascicules, as they were called, fell into disarray, and more than a century passed before anyone had any idea of how Dickinson had chosen to organize her work. Then, according to Oberhaus, something happened that restored Dickinson's own sense of order: "[T]he poet's original arrangement was not fully restored until 1981 with the publication of [Ralph W.] Franklin's *Manuscript Books of Emily Dickinson*. Guided by such evidence as stationery imperfections, smudge patterns, and puncture marks where the poet's needle had pierced the paper to bind them, Franklin returned the fascicles to their original state. For the first time, facsimiles of the forty fascicles were made available to readers in the form Dickinson had assembled them. ... Sharon Cameron…presented strong evidence that Emily Dickinson assembled the fascicles deliberately rather than chronologically. As Cameron points out, for example, some fascicles are composed of poems that Dickinson copied in different years. In some cases she later inserted an additional sheet into a fascicle she had already completed. In others she left a verso or half-sheet blank."

Having abandoned the practice of visiting others in their homes, Dickinson embraced letter writing with new zeal, preferring the quiet times to carefully compose what she wished to say, rather than being called upon to respond instantly to a remark made out of the blue by someone else. She also liked that, in writing letters, she need not concern herself with "polite conversation" that wasted her time and intellect. Best of all, Dickinson used many of her letters as a sort of sounding board for her poetry, trying out thoughts and phrases on others before committing them to a composed piece.

As anyone who has ever had to write a piece that was limited in scope and length knows, that practice made Dickinson's work less flowery and more concise. Many have observed that it was during this era that her poems began to take on the feel of a Christian hymn both in beat and syntax. Consider, for example, the following, written in 1861:

>"You're right - 'the way is narrow'
>And 'difficult the Gate' -
>And 'few there be' - Correct again -

That 'enter in - thereat' -

'Tis Costly - so are purples!
'Tis just the price of Breath -
With but the 'Discount' of the Grave -
Termed by the Brokers - 'Death'!

And after that - there's Heaven -
The Good man's - 'Dividend' -
And Bad men - 'go to Jail' -
I guess –"

This is a strange hymn, as one 21st century Dickinson fan noted: "Her tone is breezy and dismissive, even sarcastic. She adopts the language of commerce, as if life is an investment aided by brokers and paying off with dividends. The price of life, or 'Breath,' is costly – but, hey, there is this great Death discount! … It seems she is skeptical of the ultimate destination and purpose. Life itself is 'Costly,' she implies…. Just being born incurs the cost of living, 'the price' – again the financial lingo – 'of Breath.' The 'Brokers' – those men who claim knowledge and authority – are the clergy who dispense their knowledge. It is again sarcasm when she notes that another word for their 'Discount' on the cost of life's difficult investment is 'Death.' The last stanza summarily dismisses the dual destinations of Heaven, a 'Dividend' for the good, and Hell, or 'Jail' where the 'Bad men' go, with a shrug: 'I guess.' 'Yeah, whatever,' we might say. Sure."

In spite of the differences in their stations in life, Dickinson and Susan continued to discuss poetry. Emily's sister-in-law was also a gifted writer, albeit one who mostly abandoned her craft for other traditional pursuits. Among the pieces they discussed at length was 1861's "Safe in their Alabaster Chambers."

"Safe in their Alabaster Chambers -

Untouched by Morning -

and untouched by noon -

Sleep the meek members of the Resurrection,

Rafter of Satin and Roof of Stone -

Grand go the Years,

In the Crescent above them -

Worlds scoop their Arcs -

and Firmaments - row -

Diadems - drop -

And Doges surrender -

Soundless as Dots,

On a Disk of Snow."

Published anonymously in the *Springfield Republican* in March 1862, the piece remains one of a few of Dickinson's works to have been published during her lifetime. Literary scholar Helen Vendler analyzed this poem, writing, "Dickinson binds together her sequences of deaths by interwoven alliteration (first 'd' for Death, then 's,' perhaps for cessation) to emphasize their inevitability: 'Diadems drop…Doges…dots…Disc; surrender…Soundless…sow.' Just as her 'd' words – with the exception of 'drop' – include 's' ('Diadems,' 'Doges,' dots,' 'Disc'), her 's' words (except for 'snow') include 'd' ('surrender,' Soundless'). The braid of extinction is woven too tight for anyone to escape its grasp."

While it would seem from her private correspondence and works that Dickinson was more than satisfied with remaining unmarried, a related issue obviously weighed on her mind. Given her lot in life, she had to know she was being seen as an object of pity by her neighbors, who were no doubt speaking in sad, hushed tones behind her back about how she given her life to education at the expense of a husband and children. It was likely to these types of people that Dickinson addressed her "wife" poems. Written in the decade following her brother's marriage, Emily frequently wrote in these works that marriage offered women little beyond toil and distraction from higher things. For example, Emily wrote the following poem, "She rose to His Requirement," sometime around 1863:

"She rose to His Requirement – dropt
The Playthings of Her Life
To take the honorable Work
Of Woman, and of Wife -

"If ought She missed in Her new Day,
Of Amplitude, or Awe -
Or first Prospective - Or the Gold
In using, wear away,

"It lay unmentioned - as the Sea
Develope Pearl, and Weed,
But only to Himself - be known

The Fathoms they abide —"

Writing in 1979, authors Sandra M Gilbert and Susan Gubar observed of this poem, and others like it, "The fact that in some poems Dickinson analyzes this female double life of surface requirements and sea-deep pearl with surgical calm does not mean she is unsympathetic to the women who endure the psychic splits she describes. Nor does it mean that she supposed herself exempt from such problems because she never officially undertook the work of wife. On the contrary, both her irony and her objectivity were intensified by her sense that she herself was trapped in the Requirements by which all women were surrounded, a tangled set of implicit laws."

Indeed, "She rose" offers little in the way of censure when compared to the near tragic "Born—Bridalled—Shrouded."

"Title divine—is mine!

The Wife—without the Sign!

Acute Degree—conferred on me—

Empress of Calvary!

Royal—all but the Crown!

Betrothed—without the swoon

God sends us Women—

When you—hold—Garnet to Garnet—

Gold—to Gold—

Born—Bridalled—Shrouded—

In a Day—

Tri Victory

"My Husband"—women say—

Stroking the Melody—

Is this—the way?"

This poem is laden with religious symbolism, such as "title divine," "empress of Calvary," and

"God sends us women." Then there is the backhanded praise of sacrifice, for like Christ, the married woman is "shrouded," but without the hope for resurrection, at least not in this life. In the Protestant world of the 19th century, there was no respectable role for a woman other than that of wife and mother. Unlike their Catholic sisters, who might enjoy fulfilling, even powerful lives in the hierarchy of a convent or monastery, Protestant women who chose to devote their lives to anything other than the care of men were looked upon with pity at best and suspicion at worst.

By 1865, Dickinson had authored more than a thousand poems, many of them written as she struggled with her eyesight. However, she had still seen almost none of her works published, a fact that seemed to barely faze her. In April 1862, she wrote to Thomas Wentworth Higginson, the author of an article entitled "Letter to a Young Contributor" in the *Atlantic Monthly*. She sent four of her poems, along with these words:

> "Are you too deeply occupied to say if my Verse is alive?
>
> The Mind is so near itself—it cannot see, distinctly—and I have none to ask—
>
> Should you think it breathed—and had you the leisure to tell me, I should feel quick gratitude—
>
> If I make the mistake—that you dared to tell me—would give me sincerer honor—toward you—
>
> I enclose my name—asking you, if you please—Sir—to tell me what is true?
>
> That you will not betray me—it is needless to ask—since Honor is it's own pawn—"

It remains unknown if Higginson responded, but it must not have been pleasant, for she later described the changes he made to her works as "surgery." For his own part, Higginson later complained, "I foresee that 'Young Contributors' will send me worse things than ever now. Two such specimens of verse as came yesterday & day before—fortunately not to be forwarded for publication!"

Higginson

For her part, Dickinson mostly refrained from trying to get any more of her works published again. She even castigated the process in one poem:

"Publication – is the Auction

Of the Mind of Man –

Poverty – be justifying

For so foul a thing

"Possibly – but We – would rather

From Our Garret go

White – unto the White Creator –

Than invest – Our Snow –

"Thought belong to Him who gave it –

Then – to Him Who bear

It's Corporeal illustration – sell

The Royal Air –

"In the Parcel – Be the Merchant

Of the Heavenly Grace –

But reduce no Human Spirit

To Disgrace of Price –"

   Given that the specter of slave auctions haunted abolitionists in the North like little else, Dickinson's imagery her is virulent indeed, but she did have a few poems published in the 1860s and one in the 1870s. Of course, the lack of publication does not mean that her poems were going unread, for she enjoyed sending them on to friends and family members for comments and approval. This was a common practice among women authors of her social class, in an era when publicity was seen as unbecoming and women often used male pseudonyms when actually publishing a work.

   In fact, Emily's friends and family often shared her poems with others, giving her a sort of acceptable notoriety in New England's literary circles. Writing for *The Emily Dickinson Journal* in 1996, Lissa Holloway-Attaway explained, "Dickinson's numerous references to circularity in her work, not only in literal rounded forms but also in less overt circular methods of communication, are rhetorical power sources. Her resistance to linearity allows her to de-structure the hierarchical, biased, and binary codes of the patriarchal formula for success. Dickinson revolutionizes their rigid schematic which separates the world into discrete oppositional categories (male/female) and which clearly aligns women with weakness (dominant/subordinate). By privileging a model with curved and gentle lines for borders, with insides and outsides, and with holes to be traversed and filled in, Dickinson creates a complex, dangerous, and dynamic universe. Her drawing of circles, her circular logic, and her circulation of ambiguous truths demasters convention by keeping power in orbit; she defies the static demands of top-down constructions that hold woman still and confine her to one place of subservience when she evades linear logic."

Did Dickinson actually secretly desire to be published? It seems she did, but she could not admit it, even to herself. This sense of unfulfilled dreams can be seen in some of her works, such as the following:

> "Hope" is the thing with feathers -
>
> That perches in the soul -
>
> And sings the tune without the words -
>
> And never stops - at all -
>
>
> "And sweetest - in the Gale - is heard -
>
> And sore must be the storm -
>
> That could abash the little Bird
>
> That kept so many warm -
>
>
> "I've heard it in the chillest land -
>
> And on the strangest Sea -
>
> Yet - never - in Extremity,
>
> It asked a crumb - of me."

As an avid naturalist, Dickinson was only too aware that birds might come close for brief moments, but they would never stay, nor would they give warning before taking off. Likewise, a strong wind might take a bird away, even when it had no desire to go. Such was the way, it seems, that she saw hope.

Likewise, Dickinson saw life as something that was best experienced by comparison rather than direct observation. Author Shirley Sharon-Zisser quotes Dickinson as writing, "I always try to think in any disappointment that had I been gratified, it had been sadder still, and I weave from such suppositions, at times, considerable consolation; consolation upside down as I am pleased to call it…" Sharon-Zisser adds, "For Dickinson, 'any disappointment' paradoxically becomes 'at once power and paralysis.' The internal powers summoned to cope with disappointments and deprivations are presented as exercised to their full capacity and hence as becoming developed to a point in which they are of intrinsic value. Thus on the emotional level, 'Pain' can be an occasion to 'learn' the skill of 'Transport' out of the pain situation. …the failure to consummate the desire to know by means of language what lies beyond the bounds of human perception serves Dickinson as an occasion for perfecting the linguistic apparatus as an end in itself. As similes are the linguistic tool designated by Dickinson as the most adequate to sound the unknown, it is in her manipulation of similes that Dickinson's introverting reaction to the failure of this desire is...."

Dickinson herself admitted in 1863:

"We see — Comparatively —
The Thing so towering high
We could not grasp its segment
Unaided — Yesterday —

"This Morning's finer Verdict —
Makes scarcely worth the toil —
A furrow — Our Cordillera —
Our Apennine — a Knoll —

"Perhaps 'tis kindly — done us —
The Anguish — and the loss —
The wrenching — for His Firmament
The Thing belonged to us —

"To spare these striding spirits
Some Morning of Chagrin —
The waking in a Gnat's — embrace —
Our Giants — further on —"

By this time, Dickinson had completed one of her most important works, the morbid but revealing "It was not for death that I stood up."

"It was not Death, for I stood up,

And all the Dead, lie down -

It was not Night, for all the Bells

Put out their Tongues

"It was not Frost, for on my Flesh

I felt Siroccos

Nor Fire - for just my marble feet

Could keep a Chancel,

"And yet, it tasted, like them all,

The Figures I have seen

Set orderly, for Burial

Reminded me, of mine -

"As if my life were shaven,

And fitted to a frame,

And could not breathe without a key,

And 'twas like Midnight, some -

"When everything that ticked - has stopped -

And space stares - all around -

Or Grisly frosts - first Autumn morns,

Repeal the Beating Ground -

"But most, like Chaos - Stopless - cool -

Without a Chance, or sparspar The top mast of a ship -

Or even a Report of Land -

To justify - Despair."

As she moved into middle age, Dickinson wrote less and spent more time on hter other passion: gardening. During her life, those who knew her best thought of her as an avid gardener and amateur botanist, and by the 1870s, the gardens at the Homestead were the stuff of legends. Emily expanded them to include more than 400 different types of flowers, as well as other types of plants, including "carpets of lily-of-the-valley and pansies, platoons of sweetpeas, hyacinths, enough in May to give all the bees of summer dyspepsia. There were ribbons of peony hedges and drifts of daffodils in season, marigolds to distraction—a butterfly utopia." She shared her botanical wealth with others, often sending baskets of flowers to friends in times of grief or celebration.

Sadly, there was plenty of grief in Dickinson's own life during this time. She lost her beloved father on June 16, 1874, and the following year, her mother suffered a stroke that would incapacitate her for the rest of her life. At the same time, she expanded her romantic interests to include Judge Lord, to whom she wrote in 1880, "While others go to Church, I go to mine, for are you not my Church, and have we not a Hymn that no one knows but us?"

Dickinson continued to write, even as her health slowly failed. However, perhaps due to some sort of early onset dementia or other mental decline, she stopped creating her fascicules and instead just kept her poems loose, rarely editing them but instead just writing, it seems, to relieve her mind. She was so dissatisfied with her work by this point in her life that she made Lavinia promise to burn all her writings following her death.

As her own physical health began to suffer, Dickinson's last years were made all the more difficult by tragedies that struck those around her. For one thing, Austin and Susan became increasingly dissatisfied with each other, and Austin took a married editor named Mabel Loomis Todd as his mistress. Susan, devastated by what was happening, turned to the Dickinson family for comfort, driving a wedge between Austin and his family. When Emily's mother died in November 1882, she wrote to Elizabeth Holland, "Mother has now been gone five Weeks. We should have thought it a long Visit, were she coming back - Now the 'Forever' thought almost shortens it, as we are nearer rejoining her than her own return - We were never intimate Mother and Children while she was our Mother - but Mines in the same Ground meet by tunneling and when she became our Child, the Affection came - when we were Children and she journeyed, she always brought us something. Now, would she bring us but herself, what an only Gift - Memory is a strange Bell-Jubilee, and Knell."

The following year, Dickinson's favorite nephew, Austin's son Gilbert, died of typhoid fever, leaving everyone stricken with grief.

In the summer months of 1884, Emily suddenly fainted while working in the kitchen. She remained unconscious for hours, and when she awoke, she was so weak and ill that it took weeks for her to recover. Later that year, she wrote, "The Dyings have been too deep for me, and before I could raise my Heart from one, another has come."

In the year that followed, she became increasingly frail, leading the family to begin to expect the worst. By the end of 1885, she was bedridden but still managed to write some.

In the spring of 1886, Emily seemingly gathered together all her remaining energy to write a series of letters to those she loved the most. Though they did not overtly say so, she was bidding her friends and family a final farewell. On May 15, 1886, she died, most likely from Bright's disease, a form of kidney disease.

Dickinson's grave

Today, it is impossible to grow up in America without reading Emily Dickinson's poetry, and her name is instantly recognizable. Given the course of her life, and the manner in which her poetry remained almost completely unpublished, her legacy as a literary giant is almost miraculous. Fortunately for posterity, when Emily's dear sister stumbled upon the vast amount of Dickinson's poetry, she refused to grant Emily's request that it all be burned. According to Oberhaus, "After her death…[Dickinson's] sister, Lavinia—to whom she had willed all her earthly possessions—was astonished to discover the forty booklets among the poet's papers, as well as copies of nearly four hundred poems arranged in the manner of the booklets, but unbound; miscellaneous fair copies; semifinal drafts; and worksheet drafts written on odds and ends of paper—the backs of envelopes and discarded letters, bits of wrapping paper, and edges of newspapers. Lavinia, who had known her sister wrote poems but had not suspected how many, was determined they be published. First she turned for editorial help to her sister-in-law, Susan Gilbert Dickinson…When Susan failed to take action quickly enough to suit Lavinia, she retrieved the poems, then gave them to Mabel Loomis Todd…who took on the enormous task of editing the manuscripts. …Todd selected and edited several hundred poems from the mixed cache discovered by Lavinia, then saw them through their publication in the three editions of the 1890s."

The cover for the first edition of Dickinson's poems

For a woman who showed such interest in immortality, and certainly for the millions who have been blessed to read her work ever since, it was a fortuitous turn of events indeed.

Online Resources

Other books about poets by Charles River Editors

Other books about Emily Dickinson on Amazon

Bibliography

Bloom, Harold. 1999. *Emily Dickinson*. Broomall, PA: Chelsea House Publishers.

Farr, Judith (ed). 1996. *Emily Dickinson: A Collection of Critical Essays*. Prentice Hall International Paperback Editions.

Farr, Judith. 2005. *The Gardens of Emily Dickinson*. Cambridge, Massachusetts & London, England: Harvard University Press.

Grabher, Gudrun, Roland Hagenbüchle and Cristanne Miller. 1998. *The Emily Dickinson Handbook*. Amherst: University of Massachusetts Press.

Habegger, Alfred. 2001. *My Wars Are Laid Away in Books: The Life of Emily Dickinson*. New York: Random House.

Martin, Wendy (ed). 2002. *The Cambridge Companion to Emily Dickinson*. Cambridge: Cambridge University Press.

McNeil, Helen. 1986. *Emily Dickinson*. London: Virago Press.

Sewall, Richard B.. 1974. *The Life of Emily Dickinson*. New York: Farrar, Straus, and Giroux.

Wolff, Cynthia Griffin. 1986. *Emily Dickinson*. New York. Alfred A. Knopf.

Free Books by Charles River Editors

We have brand new titles available for free most days of the week. To see which of our titles are currently free, click on this link.

Discounted Books by Charles River Editors

We have titles at a discount price of just 99 cents everyday. To see which of our titles are currently 99 cents, click on this link.

Printed in Great Britain
by Amazon